Now I Kno

Bears

by MELVIN AND GILDA BERGER

SCHOLASTIC INC.
New York Toronto London Auckland Sydney
Mexico City New Delhi Hong Kong Buenos Aires

Cover: © Adam Jones / Photo Researchers, Inc.; page 1: © Adam Jones / Photo Researchers, Inc.; page 3 large: © Galen Rowell / Peter Arnold, Inc., inset: © Mark Newman / Photo Researchers, Inc.; page 4 large: © Steven Kazlowski / Peter Arnold, Inc., inset: © Roland Seitre / Peter Arnold, Inc.; page 5: © Steven Kazlowski / Peter Arnold, Inc.; page 6 left: © Steven Kazlowski / Peter Arnold, Inc., right: © Steven Kazlowski / Peter Arnold, Inc.; page 7 © D. Robert & Lorri Franz / Corbis; page 8 left: © Steven Kazlowski / Peter Arnold, Inc.; page 9: © Alan & Sandy Carey / Photo Researchers, Inc.; page 10: © John Shaw / www.bciusa.com; page 11: © Steven Kazlowski / Peter Arnold, Inc.; page 12: © Steven Kazlowski / Peter Arnold, Inc.; page 13: © Tom Murphy / WWI / Peter Arnold, Inc.; page 14: © Bruce Coleman / www.bciusa.com; page15: © Roland Seitre / Peter Arnold, Inc.; page 16: © Lynn Rogers / Peter Arnold, Inc.; page 17: © Thomas D. Mangelsen / Peter Arnold, Inc.; page 18: © Tom Murphy / WWI / Peter Arnold, Inc.; page 19: © Wayne Lankinen / www.bciusa.com; page 20: © John Serrao / Photo Researchers, Inc.; page 21: © William Ervin / Photo Researchers, Inc.; page 22: © Leonard L. Rue III / www.bciusa.com; page 23: © E & P Bauer / www.bciusa.com; page 24 © Gerard Lacz / Peter Arnold, Inc.; page 25: © Tom & Pat Leeson / Photo Researchers, Inc.; page 26: © Steven Kazlowski / Peter Arnold, Inc.; page 27 large: © Thomas D. Mangelsen / Peter Arnold, Inc., inset: © Bruce Lichtenberger / Peter Arnold, Inc.; page 28 large: © Joel Bennett / Peter Arnold, Inc., inset: © Mark Newman / www.bciusa.com; page 29 large © Alan & Sandy Carey / zefa / Corbis, inset: © Larry Allen / www.bciusa.com; page 30: © Fred Bruemmer / Peter Arnold, Inc.; page 31: © Fred Bruemmer / Peter Arnold, Inc.; page 32: © Daniel J. Cox / Corbis

ISBN 0-439-88849-2

20 19 18 17 15 16/0

Printed in the U.S.A.
First Printing, September 2006
Book design by Nancy Sabato

Bears are powerful animals.

Bears walk on all four feet.

DID YOU KNOW?

Bears stand up to look around or fight.

They can also stand up on two feet.

Most bears live where it is cold.

Their fur keeps them warm.

Some bears have very large bodies.
The grizzly bear grows very big.

It eats lots of food every day.

The biggest bear of all
is the brown bear.

The brown bear likes to eat fish.

The polar bear has a white coat.

DID YOU KNOW?

Polar bears only eat meat and fish.

It is hard to see a polar bear
in the snow.

DID YOU KNOW?

All sun bears have white or yellow chest marks.

The smallest bear is called the sun bear.

The sun bear likes to climb trees.

Most bears eat a lot in the summer.

They get big and fat.

In the winter, most bears do not eat!

DID YOU KNOW?

Bears snore when they sleep.

They sleep all winter in caves or hollow logs.

Sometimes a bear wakes up
and looks outside.

If it is not too cold, the bear may go out and look for a winter snack!

DID YOU KNOW?

Baby bears are called cubs.

Baby bears are born during the winter.

They are small, with very little fur.

The cubs stay close to their mother.

They also like to have fun!

The mother bear takes
good care of her cubs.

She teaches them how to find food.

The mother polar bear teaches her cubs how to swim.

The mother black bear teaches her cubs how to climb trees.

Most cubs stay with their mother for about two years.

Then — away they go!

GLOSSARY

Bears: Large, heavy animals with thick fur.

Black bear: A smaller kind of bear. Black bears may have brown or white fur.

Brown bear: A very big bear. Brown bears are the largest bears in the world.

Cave: A large hole under the ground or in the side of a hill.

Cub: A young bear. Most bear cubs are born in winter.

Fur: The hairy coat of an animal. The fur of most bears is long and soft.

Grizzly: A kind of brown bear. A grizzly bear has some white hairs in its brown fur.

Polar bear: A large bear that lives around the North Pole. A polar bear's fur is either white or yellow.

Sun bear: The smallest kind of bear in the world. A sun bear climbs trees to find honey and insects.